What's it like to be... a BEE ?

Jinny Johnson

illustrated by **Desiderio Sanzi**

W
FRANKLIN WATTS
LONDON•SYDNEY

An Appleseed Editions book

First published in 2013 by Franklin Watts
338 Euston Road, London NW1 3BH

© 2011 Appleseed Editions

Created by Appleseed Editions Ltd,
Well House, Friars Hill, Guestling,
East Sussex TN35 4ET

Designed and illustrated by Guy Callaby
Edited by Mary-Jane Wilkins

ISBN 978 1 4451 2188 8

Dewey Classification: 595.7'99

A CIP catalogue for this book is available
from the British Library.

Printed in China

Franklin Watts is a division of
Hachette Children's Books,
an Hachette UK company.
www.hachette.co.uk

Contents

A bee is an insect.
It has six legs and two
pairs of wings.

So what's it like to be a bee?

I'm a busy honeybee.

Do you like my stripes?

I live with lots
of other bees.

We make a nest
in a hole in a tree.

Our mum is called the
queen bee.

She is bigger than
the rest of us.

She lays all the eggs for our family.

An egg

A queen bee can lay 2,500 eggs in a day.

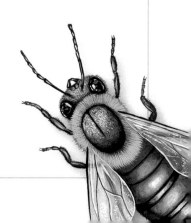

I began life as an egg.

I hatched into a little wiggly creature called a larva.

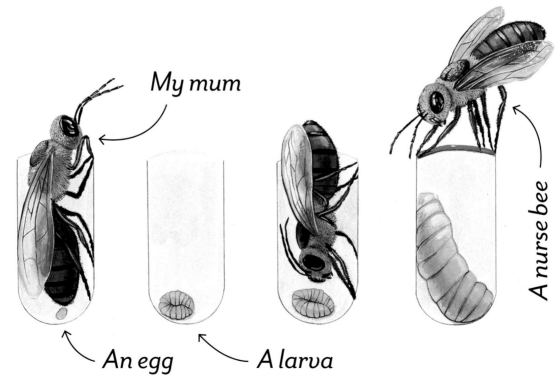

My mum

An egg

A larva

A nurse bee

I grew very quickly.

It takes just three weeks for a bee to grow to full size.

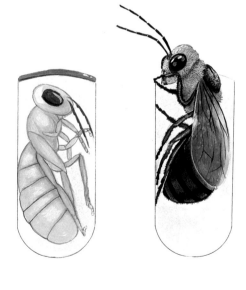

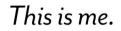

This is me.

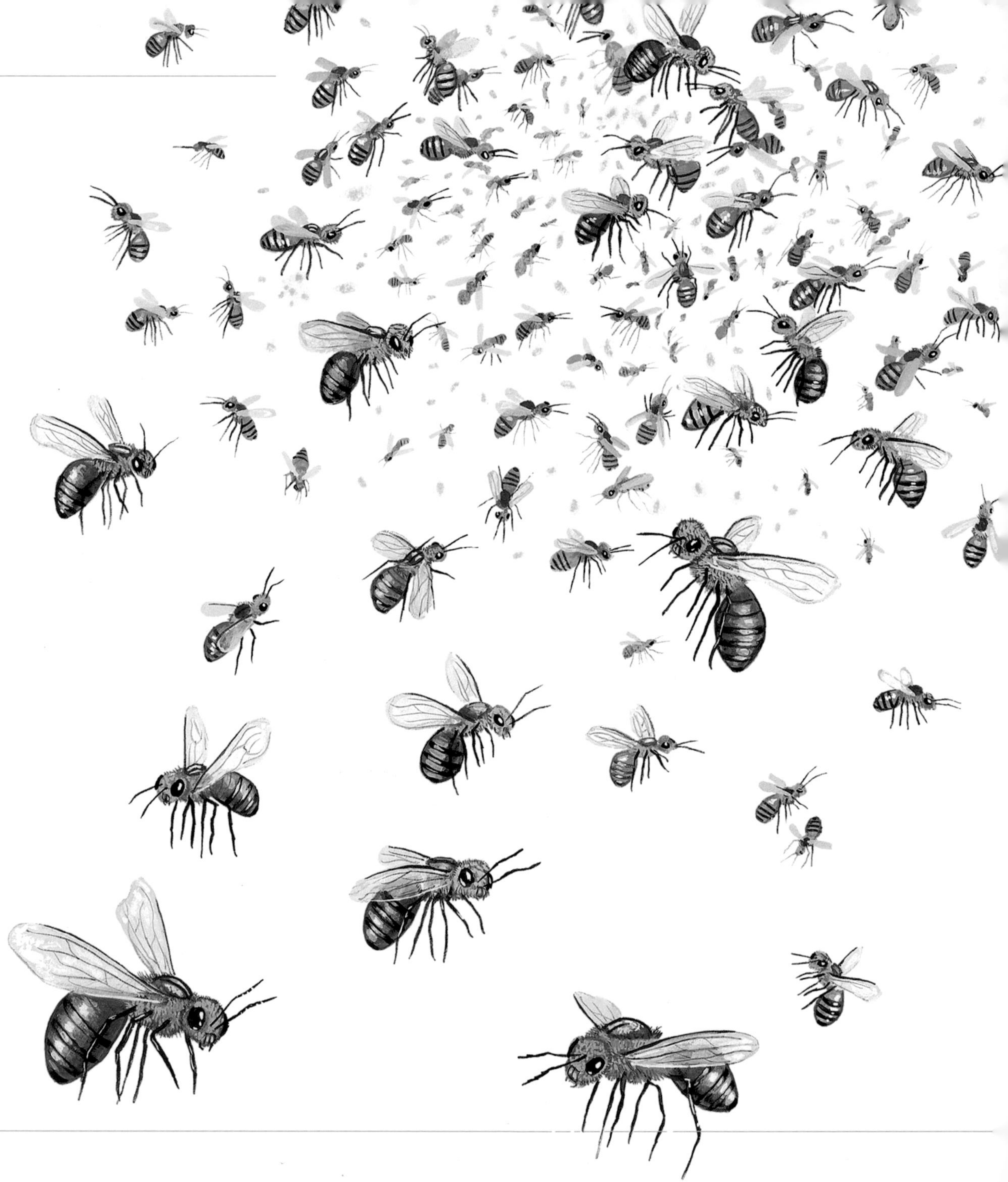

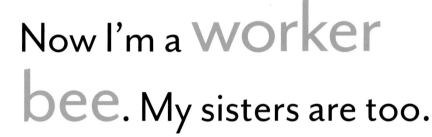

Now I'm a worker bee. My sisters are too. We look after our home and find food for us all.

Every morning I fly out
to find food.

buzz, buzz, buzz

A bee's wings
beat 200 times
a second.

First, I look for some flowers.

There is a sweet sticky liquid inside flowers.

This is called nectar.

These clover flowers have lots of nectar.

I suck up the nectar
with my long tongue.

*Can you see
my tongue
starting to
poke out?*

I collect a yellow dust
from flowers too.

This is called pollen.

Can you see the ball of pollen on my leg?

A honeybee carries pollen on little hairs on her back legs.

I take the nectar and pollen back to the nest.

We use the pollen to make food for the baby bees in our family.

This is a baby bee.

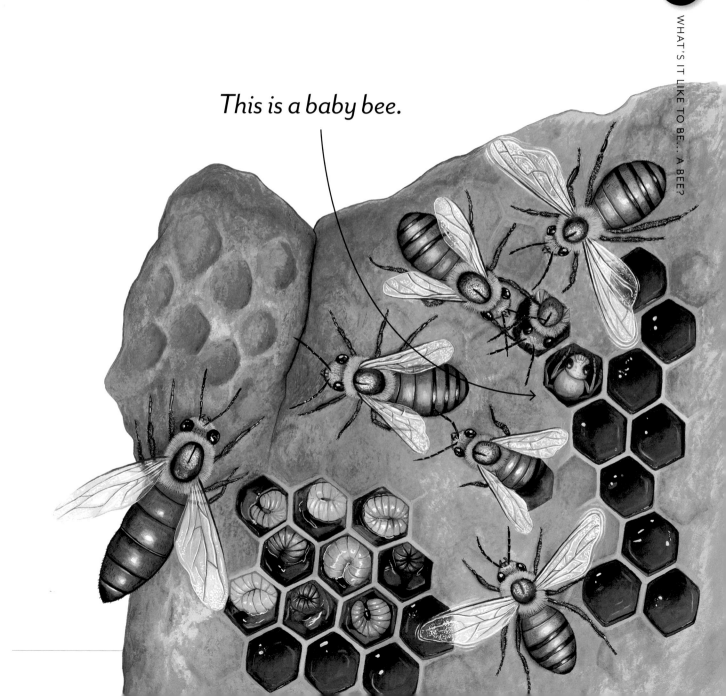

We put the nectar into special little pots in our nest.

It turns into honey.

We eat the honey in winter.

It takes 556 bees to make enough honey for one jar.

More about bees

Why do bees sting?

A bee only stings if it's very scared or if someone is attacking it or its home. The sting is a sharp spike at the end of its body. A bee usually dies after it stings.

What do bees eat if we take their honey?

Bees make more honey than they need. Bee-keepers only take some of the honey and leave the bees plenty to eat.

What do bees do in winter?

Bees don't like to go out when it's cold. So they stay in the hive and huddle together to keep warm. They eat the honey they have made.

How do bees make their nest?

Bees build the inside of their nest with wax. The bees make the wax in their own bodies.

Bee words

larva
A baby bee.

nectar
*A sweet liquid
inside flowers.*

nurse bee
*A worker bee that looks
after baby bees in the nest.*

pollen
*Fine yellow powder
on flowers that helps the
plant make new plants.*

queen bee
*Head of a bee family.
The queen lays all
the eggs.*

worker bee
*A bee that gathers food,
helps build the nest and
looks after the family.*

Bee index